Dance, Sing, Remember

A Celebration of Jewish Holidays

Leslie Kimmelman
illustrated by Ora Eitan

HarperCollins*Publishers*

Special thanks to Rabbi William Dreskin of Woodlands Community Temple
in New York for his many insightful comments

Dance, Sing, Remember: *A Celebration of Jewish Holidays*
Text copyright © 2000 by Leslie Kimmelman. Illustrations copyright © 2000 by Ora Eitan.
Printed in the U.S.A. All rights reserved. www.harperchildrens.com

Library of Congress Cataloging-in-Publication Data
Kimmelman, Leslie.
  Dance, sing, remember : a celebration of Jewish holidays / Leslie Kimmelman ; illustrated by Ora Eitan.
    p.   cm.
  Summary: Explains eleven major Jewish holidays and how they are celebrated.
  ISBN 0-06-027725-4. — ISBN 0-06-027726-2 (lib. bdg.)
  1. Fasts and feasts—Judaism—Juvenile literature. [1. Fasts and feasts—Judaism. 2. Judaism—Customs and practices.] I. Eitan, Ora,
1940– ill. II. Title.
BM690.K495 2000   98-12699
296.4'3—dc21   CIP
                                                                                  AC

1 2 3 4 5 6 7 8 9 10 ❖ First Edition

To my mother—who makes the world's tenderest brisket,
tastiest hamantaschen, and most tantalizing chicken soup—with love
—L.K.

To my beloved parents, who give each day the flavor of a holiday
—O.E.

CONTENTS

Hag Sameach!

Happy Holidays!

The Jewish religion is thousands of years old. For all those years, month after month, Jewish people all over the world have been celebrating special days. Some of these holidays are happy; others are sad. Some are happy and sad at the same time. A few have been celebrated for only a short time, and some have been celebrated for centuries. But every holiday is a way of remembering, a way of connecting children to their parents and grandparents and to _their_ parents and grandparents—all the way back to the very first Jews.

Kiss the mezzuzah. Come in! Shalom! A whole year of Jewish holidays is beginning.

1

Rosh Hashanah
ראש השנה

First come the High Holy Days—the holiest days of the year. Rosh Hashanah, which means "the head of the year," is the Jewish New Year. It takes place in late summer or early fall.

2

On Rosh Hashanah, we light the holiday candles and bless the wine and the round loaf of *challah*. We dip challah and apples in honey. *"Shanah Tovah,"* we say—a sweet new year. After dinner, and the next day, too, it's time for synagogue. At synagogue, we listen to the blowing of the *shofar*, a long, twisty trumpet made from the horn of a sheep. *Sshhh!* Hear its long, loud sounds. It's telling everyone the new year has begun. We hope it will be even happier than the year that just ended.

Yom Kippur
יום כפור

Ten days after Rosh Hashanah, it's Yom Kippur, the Day of Atonement. Yom Kippur means no school, no work, no playing—and for grown-ups, no eating. Instead, we bring boxes and cans of food to synagogue for people who don't have enough money to buy food for themselves. Inside the crowded synagogue, we listen to the sad, sweet music of the cantor and to the prayers of the rabbi. To start the year off right, we atone for the bad things we've done. We say "I'm sorry" to friends and family whose feelings we've hurt. We promise God and each other to try harder and do better.

Sshhh! Listen as the shofar is blown again. The loud, happy blasts tell everyone that the High Holy Days, which began with Rosh Hashanah, are over.

Jonah and the Great Fish

Every Yom Kippur, the story of Jonah is read at synagogue. It is a story about making mistakes and learning from them, and about asking for forgiveness.

There once was a city named Nineveh. Terrible things were happening there. The people who lived in Nineveh had forgotten all about God. They had forgotten about being good people and leading good lives. God was very angry. God told Jonah to go to Nineveh and to warn everyone of God's anger.

Jonah did not want to go. So he ran away. He hid on a ship that was sailing far, far away. After a few days at sea, there was a terrible storm. The waves were so big, and the wind was so strong, that the little ship was in danger of sinking.

"God must be angry with someone on our ship," the sailors said.

Then Jonah said, "I am the one who has made God angry. If you throw me into the sea, the storm will stop."

So the sailors threw Jonah overboard, and the sea was calm again.

But an enormous fish swallowed Jonah whole. For three days, inside the belly of that fish, Jonah prayed for forgiveness. God heard his prayers and made the big fish spit Jonah out on the land.

Again God told Jonah to go to Nineveh. This time Jonah

obeyed. The people of Nineveh listened to Jonah. When they heard that God was angry with them, they promised to change their ways. Just like Jonah, they prayed to God for forgiveness. And God forgave them.

This made Jonah mad. He had come so far, and now God wasn't even going to punish Nineveh. He sat outside town, shaded from the sun by a big plant, thinking angry thoughts about God. So God decided to teach Jonah a lesson. God made the plant die. The hot sun beat down on Jonah. Jonah felt sad for the plant and very sorry for himself.

God said to Jonah: "You feel sad about the green plant, and you feel sorry for yourself. Don't you think I should feel sad about the many, many people who live in Nineveh, and forgive them, and help them to change?"

Jonah learned something important that day: Just as God will forgive anyone who tries to do better, so, too, people must learn to forgive each other.

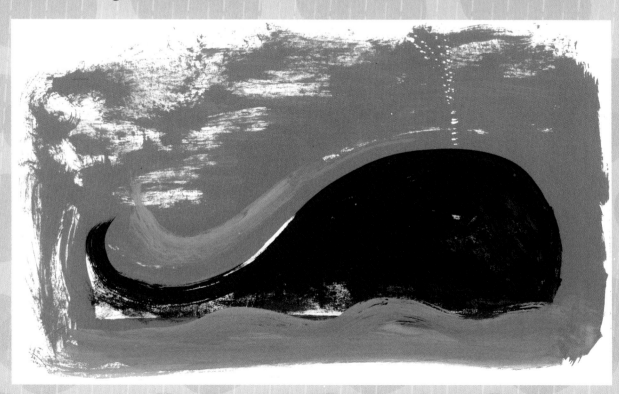

Sukkot

סוכות

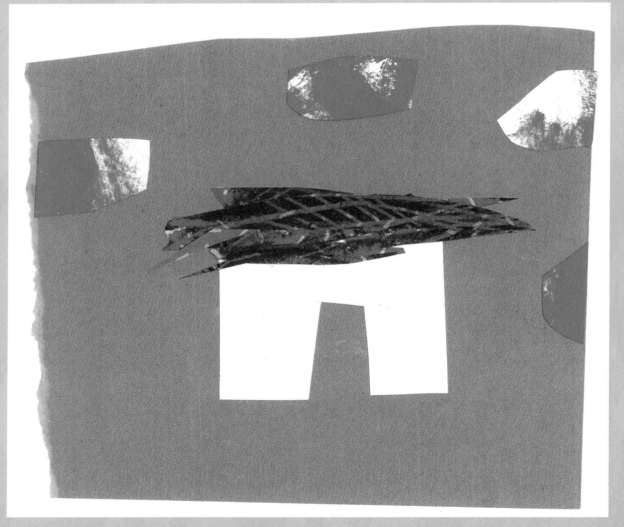

Sukkot is a harvest holiday. It comes after the High Holy Days have ended. *Sukkot* means "booths" or "huts."

Look in the backyard. The little house we've built there is called a *sukkah*. It has three walls, and a roof made out of leafy branches. Inside, fruits and vegetables and other decorations are hung. Long ago, the Jews wandered in the desert for forty years. They built little huts—*sukkot*—to live in. Later, Jewish farmers also built sukkot so they could stay near their fields at harvest time.

Every year, during the seven days of Sukkot, we remember those long-ago times. Just as the Jewish farmers did, we build a little hut to live in. We thank God for the good food of the earth, and for the rain that helps it to grow. We smell the *etrog*, a fruit that looks like a big lemon. We shake the *lulav* branches east, south, west, north, up, and down, to show that God is everywhere. Finally we eat dinner under the stars, in our little sukkah.

Harvest Muffins

Here is a recipe you can make to celebrate the fruits and vegetables of Sukkot. Make sure a grown-up helps you.

To make Harvest Muffins you will need:

2 eggs	1 large carrot, grated
⅓ cup oil	1 cup flour
¾ cup sugar	1 tsp. baking soda
1 tsp. vanilla	1 tsp. cinnamon
1 cup applesauce	¼ cup raisins
1 apple, peeled and chopped into small pieces	¼ cup mini chocolate chips

To make the muffins:

1. Preheat oven to 350°F. Grease muffin cups.
2. Beat eggs together, then stir in oil, sugar, and vanilla.
3. Mix in applesauce, apple, and carrot.
4. Add flour, baking soda, and cinnamon, stirring briefly.
5. Gently stir in raisins and chocolate chips.
6. Spoon into muffin cups, filling each cup about ¾ full.
7. Bake for 20–25 minutes, or until golden brown.

This recipe makes 12 muffins. They are delicious when served warm.

Simchat Torah

שמחת תורה

As soon as Sukkot is over, it's Simchat Torah. In synagogue every week, we read from a special book called the Torah. The Torah tells the story of how God created the world. It tells the story of Abraham and Sarah, who were the first Jews, and of the many Jewish people who came after them. And inside the Torah are all the commandments from

God to help us live as good Jews and good people. It takes
exactly one year to read the Torah from beginning to end.
Simchat Torah is the time when the rabbi finishes reading—
and immediately starts at the beginning again. There's a big
party at synagogue. The grown-ups carry the Torah scrolls
around the room seven times in a big parade. The children
carry flags. Everyone dances and sings and kisses the scrolls. It
is a celebration, a *simchat*, of the Torah.

Hanukkah

חנוכה

The eight nights of Hanukkah come next. More than two thousand years ago, there lived a Syrian king named Antiochus. He ordered the Jewish people to pray to *his* gods or face terrible punishment. Some Jews were afraid, and they obeyed. But Judah Maccabee, his father and brothers, and many other Jews refused. For three long years, they fought for the freedom to pray to their own God in their own way. The Maccabees finally won, but when they went inside the Jerusalem Temple to pray, they saw that everything was smashed and broken. Legend says there was only enough oil to light the Temple's lamp for one night. Then a miracle happened: The oil burned and burned for eight days and eight nights, filling the Temple with its beautiful brightness.

Today at Hanukkah, we celebrate the freedom to follow the Jewish religion, and we celebrate the miracle of the oil. On the first night of Hanukkah, the "Festival of Lights," we use the helper, or *shammash*, candle to light one other candle in the *menorah*, the candleholder. On the second night, the shammash lights two candles, and by the last night eight flames flicker and burn with the shammash. At Hanukkah we give gifts to family and friends. We fry potato pancakes—*latkes*—and jelly doughnuts—*sufganiyot*—in oil. And we spin dreidels round and round in a holiday game.

The Dreidel Game

The dreidel game is easy to play!

Make a big pile of pennies in the middle of the floor. Make small equal piles in front of each player, too. Then take turns spinning the dreidel.

If it lands with the Hebrew letter nun נ facing up, the player gets nothing and puts in nothing.

If the dreidel has the letter gimmel ג facing up, the player takes everything in the center pile.

If hay ה faces up, the player takes half of the center pile.

And if shin ש is faceup, the player must put two pennies from his own pile into the middle. The person with the most pennies at the end of the game is the winner.

Together, the letters on the dreidel stand for the first letters of the Hebrew words Nes gadol hayah sham: "A great miracle happened there."

In Israel, the last letter on the dreidel is different—po פ— and the dreidel reads "A great miracle happened here."

Tu B'Shevat

ט״ו בשבט

Tu B'Shevat means "the new year of the trees." In Israel, where many Jews live, the land is dry. Growing trees and other plants is very important. So Israelis celebrate Tu B'Shevat by planting new trees in their land. Jewish people all over the world help celebrate by sending money to Israel for tree planting. Sometimes we even plant a tree in our own yard in honor of the holiday. Planting trees reminds us to take good care of the Earth, our home.

And what foods are eaten on Tu B'Shevat? The delicious foods that grow on Israeli trees: olives, dates, almonds, carobs, figs, and pomegranates.

Planting Parsley

In honor of Tu B'Shevat, it's fun to plant something green.

What you need:

small pot

handful of pebbles or gravel

potting soil (mixed with a little sand, if available)

parsley seeds

What you do:

1. Place pebbles at bottom of pot. Fill most of way up with soil.
2. Press just a few seeds gently into soil; cover with about ¼" of soil.
3. Put in sunny spot, and water when needed to keep soil slightly moist.
4. Seeds should start sprouting in 2–3 weeks.

You can use some of the parsley later in spring, during the holiday of Passover.

Purim

פורים

Get ready for a party! It's Purim, the noisiest, happiest holiday of the year.

The Bible says that in the days of King Ahasueros, there lived a wicked man named Haman. When the Jews refused to bow down to Haman, saying that they bowed only before God, Haman was very angry. He convinced the king to pass a law ordering that all the Jews in the land be killed. The king did not know that his own queen was Jewish.

Queen Esther bravely went to the king, her husband, and asked him to change the law. King Ahasueros loved his queen. He realized the law was a bad one. Haman was punished, and the Jews were allowed to live in peace.

Today at Purim, there's a big costume party at synagogue. We hear the story of Esther from a special book called the *Megillah*. Each time Haman's name is spoken, we boo or stomp our feet or shake our noisy *groggers*. No one wants to hear Haman's name. Cookies called *hamantaschen* are baked for the holiday. They have three sides, just like Haman's hat. And at Purim we give *mishloach manot*, baskets of food, to friends and family and to people in need.

Groggers

Grogger means noisemaker.

What you need:

two small paper plates	*yarn*
markers or crayons	*stapler*
felt or colored paper	*dried beans (the bigger*
glue	*varieties work best)*
	Popsicle stick

What you do:

1. On one of the plates draw Queen Esther's face with your markers or crayons. Then make her crown. You can decorate it using felt or colored paper, if you like. Glue on yarn for hair. Or, if you'd rather, make Haman's face.

2. Have a grown-up staple the two plates together most of the way around.

3. Into the opening that remains, pour in about 1 cup of dried beans. Then insert the end of the Popsicle stick so that it can be used as a handle. Have the grown-up staple the opening shut.

4. Shake away—the noisier, the better!

Passover
פסח

In the spring, it's time to celebrate Passover, or *Pesach* in Hebrew.

At the holiday dinner, the *Seder*, we read the story of Passover from a book called the *Haggadah*. Thousands of years ago, cruel pharaohs ruled over the land of Egypt. The Jewish people were their slaves. They had barely enough food to eat or time to sleep. They prayed for the day when they would be free.

At last their prayers were answered. God sent the Jewish slaves a leader named Moses. Moses asked Pharaoh to let his people go. But Pharaoh's heart was hard, and he said no. So, with God's help, Moses punished Pharaoh with ten plagues. The skies turned dark during one plague; the streets filled with frogs during another. But the last plague was the worst. The oldest son in each Egyptian family became sick and died, but the sickness *passed over* the houses where Jewish families lived. When his own son died, Pharaoh finally freed the slaves.

The Jews followed Moses out of Egypt quickly, afraid that Pharaoh might change his mind. They did not even wait for their bread to rise.

Today, for the seven or eight days of Passover, we eat flat, crunchy bread called *matzah*. We dip parsley in salt water to remind us of the slaves' salty tears. We eat other special foods at the seder, too, to recall the days when we were slaves. After dinner, the children hunt for the *afikomen*, a piece of matzah that has been wrapped in a napkin and hidden. Finally, at the seder's end, we open the door for the prophet Elijah, who, Jews believe, will arrive one day to announce a time of peace in the world. Most of all, at Passover, we celebrate freedom. Someday, we pray, everyone in the world will be free.

Matzah

When Moses led the Jewish people out of Egypt, there was no time to wait for their bread to rise. It became flat, crunchy matzah.

Try making some matzah yourself! For the Passover matzah, it must be made from special Passover flour and be ready for the oven in 18 minutes. If you want, set a timer, and see if you can finish mixing and rolling before the timer dings. Or just have fun, and don't worry if it takes a little longer.

To make matzah, you will need:

1 lb. flour

¾ cup water, approximately

Preheat oven to 500°. Put flour into a bowl and slowly add water, mixing with a spoon and then your hands. Turn onto a flat surface and keep kneading with your hands until dough is firm. With a rolling pin, roll about half of dough at a time into a big circle (or any other shape), very thin. Prick all over with a fork. Bake on ungreased cookie sheet for 10–15 minutes, or until lightly golden.

The Seder Plate

The Seder Plate, which is used at Passover, has five sections. Each section represents something related to the Passover story:

ZEROAH זרוע

The lamb bone. This represents the Passover sacrifice. Lamb's blood was used by the Jews to mark the doors of their houses so that the sickness of the tenth plague would pass over them.

BETZAH ביצה

A roasted or hard-boiled egg. The betzah represents the spring, which is the season in which Moses led his people to freedom.

MAROR מרור

Bitter herbs, such as horseradish. These represent the bitterness of slavery.

HAROSET חרסת

An apple, nut, and wine mixture. This mixture represents the cementlike mixture that the slaves used to build buildings for the pharaoh.

KARPAS כרפס

Greens, usually parsley. Karpas also represents the spring.

יום השואה

Soon after Passover is a very serious and sad day on the Jewish calendar. It is called Yom Hashoah.

Not too many years ago lived an evil and powerful man, the leader of a big country. Like Haman, he wanted to kill the Jewish people. His name was Adolf Hitler. This time, he was even more powerful. This time, there was no Queen Esther to change his mind. There was no Queen Esther to help save the Jews.

On Yom Hashoah, we say prayers and remember all the Jews who died in the Holocaust, the *Shoah*. Never again can the world let such a terrible thing happen.

Yom Ha-atzma'ut

יום העצמאות

Wave a flag! Dance the *hora*! It's Yom Ha-atzma'ut, Israel's birthday!

Too often in history, Jews have been treated badly, or have been chased from the lands in which they live. That is why the Jewish people created the country of Israel. Jews from all over the world can come and live there.

Today, Israel is more than fifty years old. The Jews of Israel, and Jews who live elsewhere, all celebrate Israel's birthday together. It is good to have a safe home for the Jewish people.

The Hora

A popular dance in Israel is called the hora. People do the hora on many happy occasions. Here is how you dance the hora:

1. Gather all your friends and family and make a big circle. Now hold hands with the people on either side of you, or put your hands on their shoulders.
2. Step to the right with your right foot.
3. Step behind your right foot with your left foot.
4. Step to the right again with your right foot.
5. Hop on your right foot, kicking the left foot in front.
6. Step to the left with your left foot, and hop on it, kicking your right foot front.
7. After you've moved to the right a few times, change directions and move the circle left.

For fun, half of the dancers can form a smaller circle inside the first. Then have the two circles move in opposite directions!

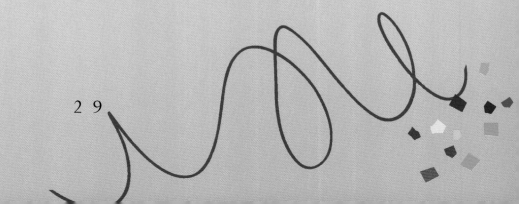

Shavuot

שבועות

Shavuot, which arrives with the warm weather, is part of the Passover story too. After Moses led the Jews out of Egypt, they came to a big mountain, Mount Sinai. Moses climbed up. At the top of the mountain God gave Moses the Torah for him to pass to his people. Shavuot celebrates the giving, and the accepting, of the Torah.

Shavuot also celebrates the first harvest of the spring. We eat lots of food with milk and cheese, such as blintzes, and honey cake. We remember that the Torah is sweet, like honey, and nourishing, like milk.

The Ten Commandments

God gave Moses and the Jewish people many important rules to live by. The ones that we know best are called the Ten Commandments. They are:

1. There is only one God.
2. Do not make any pictures or statues of God.
3. Do not take God's name in vain.
4. Remember the Sabbath, and keep it holy.
5. Honor your mother and father.
6. Do not kill.
7. Husbands and wives should be true to each other.
8. Do not steal.
9. Do not lie.
10. Do not be jealous of your neighbors or friends, or of what they have.

Shabbat
שבת

Shabbat shalom! Welcome, Sabbath—or in Hebrew, Shabbat—which comes not just once a year, but every single week.

The Torah says that God created the world—the sun and moon and the Earth, day and night, animals and people—in six days. Then God saw that the work was good, and rested on the seventh day.

So on the seventh day, we rest, too, from sundown on Friday to sundown on Saturday. We honor God with Shabbat. On Friday night, we light the candles, bless the wine and the challah, and eat a delicious dinner. Often we go to synagogue. On Saturday, we spend time thinking about the week that has just ended and the one that is about to begin. Finally, when three stars can be seen in the night sky, it is time to say good-bye to the Sabbath with the *havdalah* ("separation") ceremony. We light a special candle, bless the wine again, smell the sweet Sabbath spices, and put out the candle. The holiday has ended, but a little bit of Shabbat peace—Shabbat shalom—will be carried inside us until Shabbat begins again the next week.

Shabbat Shalom!

bim bam bim bi bi bam bim bi bi bim bim bam

Sha - bat sha - lom (clap) Sha - bat sha - lom (clap) Sha - bat Sha - bat Sha - bat Sha - bat sha-lom (clap)

Sha-bat Sha-bat Sha - bat Sha - bat sha - lom Sha-bat Sha-bat Sha-bat Sha - bat sha - lom

D.S.

Arrangement of "Shabbat Shalom" by Naftali Frankel and Sholom Secunda, based on an old Hasidic melody

A Blessing for Children

On Shabbat and on other special occasions, many parents gather their children close and bless them with these words:

Y'varech'cha adonai v'yishm'recha.

Yaer adonai panav elecha vikhuneka.

Yisa adonai panav elecha, v'yasem le'cha shalom.

May God bless you and keep you.

May God's light shine on you and be gracious to you.

May God's face be lifted upon you and give you peace.